MODERN WORLD NATIONS

Iceland

Roger K. Sandness
South Dakota State University

and

Charles F. Gritzner
South Dakota State University

CHELSEA HOUSE
P U B L I S H E R S
A Haights Cross Communications Company

Philadelphia

Frontispiece: Flag of Iceland

Cover: glacier, Jokulsarton.

CHELSEA HOUSE PUBLISHERS

VP, NEW PRODUCT DEVELOPMENT Sally Cheney
DIRECTOR OF PRODUCTION Kim Shinners
CREATIVE MANAGER Takeshi Takahashi
MANUFACTURING MANAGER Diann Grasse

Staff for ICELAND

EXECUTIVE EDITOR Lee Marcott
PRODUCTION ASSISTANT Megan Emery
PICTURE RESEARCHER 21st Century Publishing and Communications, Inc.
SERIES DESIGNER Takeshi Takahashi
COVER DESIGNER Terry Mallon
LAYOUT 21st Century Publishing and Communications, Inc.

A Haights Cross Communications ⟡ Company

http://www.chelseahouse.com

First Printing

1 3 5 7 9 8 6 4 2

Library of Congress Cataloging-in-Publication Data applied for.

ISBN 0-7910-7232-0

Table of Contents

Iceland

Perched on the northernmost rim of the inhabited world, Iceland is a country of remarkable beauty and starkly contrasting landscapes. A fine example is the glacier at Jokulsarton, which lies about 175 miles (280 kilometers) southeast of Iceland's capital, Reykjavik.

1

Iceland: A Unique Land and People

The spring was an extremely cold one. Floki climbed a certain high mountain, and north across the mountain range he could see a fjord full of drift ice. That's why they called the country Iceland. . .
—BOOK OF SETTLEMENTS (C. 1275)

By almost any measure, Iceland is one of the world's most unique lands. It is a remote, far northern island country that holds many mysteries and contradictions. Physically, it is a land whose features have been shaped and reshaped by the opposing agents of fire and ice. Its first inhabitants were Irish monks who sought seclusion on the island during the eighth century, a little more than 1,200 years ago, making Iceland one of the world's youngest countries in terms of earliest settlement. Even so, the country's parliament, the *Althing* (also *Althingi, Alping, Alpingi*), is believed to be the world's oldest government body still functioning. In another seeming contradiction, Iceland's people have achieved one of the world's highest standards of living, even though they have done so in an environment that offers many more challenges than it does useful resources. The small, 39,769-square-mile (103,000 square kilometers) island is precariously perched at the northern edge of the inhabited world, and no national capital is located farther north than Iceland's political center and largest city, Reykjavik.

Even the country's name is a contradiction: of the two large islands lying in the northern Atlantic Ocean between the shores of North America and northwestern Europe, nearly all of *Green*land is buried beneath a huge mass of deep glacial ice, while *Ice*land is the one bathed by warm ocean currents that begin in tropical latitudes. This branch of the Gulf Stream keeps the island many degrees warmer than one would expect for its location hugging the Arctic Circle. In fact, nearly 90 percent of the island is ice-free and green much of the year. Iceland's early settlers found an island largely covered by lush meadows dotted with stands of birch, willow, and other hardy trees. Even so, no other *country* has more of its area, about 12 percent, covered by glacial ice (Greenland and Antarctica are not countries). And no country of comparable size has less of its area suited to farming.

Location is extremely important to a country's development, and, generally speaking, the more remote a country, the more isolated its people are from the diffusion (flow) of materials and ideas. Iceland is one of Earth's most isolated lands. Europe's northwestern shores lie to the east more than 500 miles (800 kilometers) across the open waters of the North Atlantic; 180 miles (290 kilometers) to the west lies ice-covered Greenland and its 60,000 residents; and the barren shores of Canada's Newfoundland lie more than 1,200 miles (1,930 kilometers) to the southwest.

However, Icelanders have defied the laws of isolation. In fact, they have developed a way of life that in many respects is

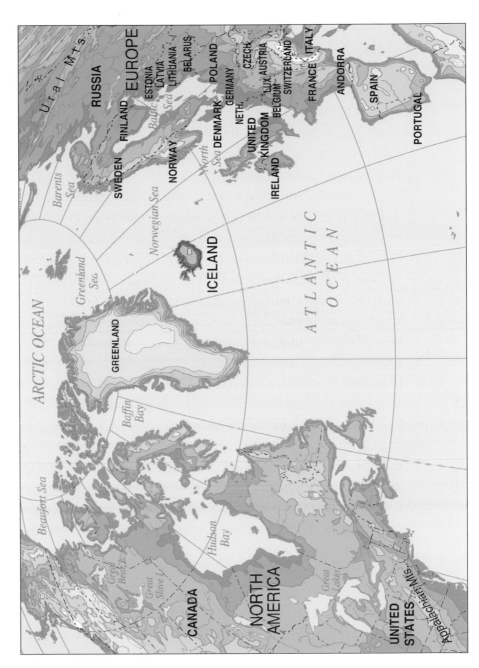

Iceland is one of the world's most remote countries, situated between the North
Atlantic and the Norwegian Sea, more than 500 miles (805 kilometers) from
Europe and 180 miles (290 kilometers) from Greenland. Despite this isolation,
Icelanders have established high standards of living and education.

one of the finest in the world. Isolation has been minimized in several ways and distance no longer limits communications. Destinations in North America and Europe are a short and relatively inexpensive hop away on the nation's international airline, Icelandair. Icelanders rank first in the world in per capita ownership and use of mobile phones and in use of the Internet. They can also boast of publishing, purchasing, and reading more books per person than any modern world nation.

Economically, Iceland is a modern "welfare state" in which its 286,000 people receive many benefits funded by the government. The cost of this is high; taxes take about half of all earned income. In return, however, Icelanders enjoy free health care, free education from preschool through university level, and a guaranteed retirement pension. Wealth is spread quite evenly through the population, and despite being Europe's most expensive country (and one of the most expensive in the world), Iceland has little poverty. Crime of any kind, particularly crime of a violent nature, is almost unknown. Among the world's countries, Iceland ranks fifth in per capita wealth and fifth in life expectancy, and is the fifth-least corrupt. The country's literacy rate of 99.9 percent is the world's highest, and no other country can match its high percentage of school-age children who actually attend school. With statistics such as these, it is little wonder that, according to the United Nations Human Development Report, Iceland is the fifth best country in the world in which to live!

Iceland boasts many firsts. In 1703, it conducted the first national census of the modern era. In 1980, it became the first modern world nation to freely elect a woman as head of state (She was so popular, in fact, that she was reelected to three additional four-year terms!). Iceland ranks first in the harnessing and use of geothermal energy. In fact, it is working to become the first country in the world to free itself from dependence on fossil fuels. Perhaps less praiseworthy, Iceland also ranks first in the per capita consumption of cola soft drinks!

Yes, in countless ways, Iceland is a fascinating, mysterious, contradictory land. It is a rugged land where dairy cattle must wear "bras" to protect their udders from the sharp volcanic rocks; it is a country where people swim outdoors during winter months in Arctic pools heated by geothermal springs; and, despite its small population, it is a country that boasts a Nobel Prize-winner in literature (Halldor Laxness, 1955) and one of the world's most famous pop singers (Björk). This book will take you on a journey of this marvelous country. You will wander through its unique past and tour its present-day regions and cities. You will meet the Icelanders and learn of their way of life, government, and economy. You will visit sites that reveal why Iceland is so often referred to as a "land of fire and ice." Welcome to Iceland—a unique land and people!

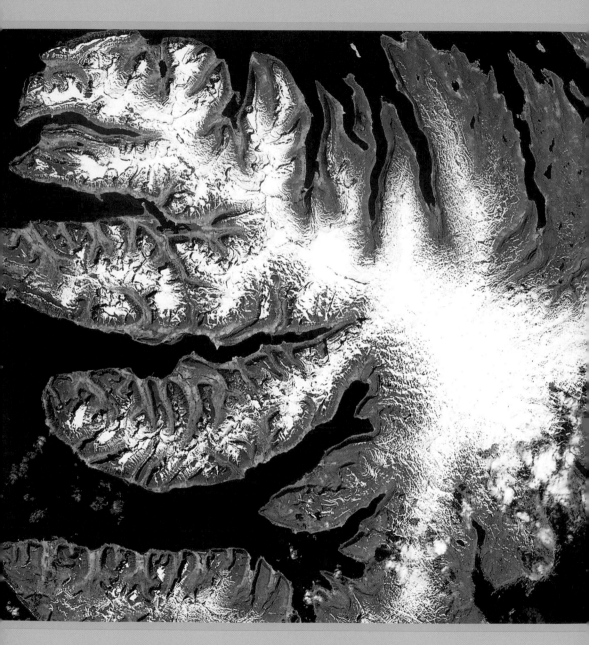

As this satellite image shows, Iceland's shores are anything but smooth. Built by volcanic activity and sculpted by the powerful forces of ice and sea, the rugged landscape of the Western Fjords forms a large portion of Iceland's coastline.

2

Landscapes of Fire and Ice

Iceland's physical geography can be summarized in three words: fire, ice, and sea. The island country rose from the sea as molten volcanic material. Today, approximately one-eighth of Iceland remains buried under glacial ice or permanent snow cover, but volcanic activity continues to be an omnipresent threat to the island's people and property. As in the past, the population still depends heavily on the sea for things as far ranging as the relatively mild climate and the variety of marine resources to support the economy.

On first glance, it would seem that few countries have less to offer its residents than does Iceland. Yet in few other lands have people better adapted to their natural environment, or taken greater advantage of what nature has to offer. Located near the Arctic Circle and relatively small in area (about the size of Virginia), Iceland has very limited productive land. About 79 percent of the island is classified as wasteland, covered by glaciers, snowfields, desert, lava flows, mountains, or urban settlement. Approximately 20 percent of its area is pastureland, which supports Iceland's thriving live-stock grazing industry. Only about 1 percent of the country is suitable for the growing of such hearty crops as hay, potatoes, and turnips. In this chapter, you will learn about Iceland's physical conditions and how they have proven to be both hazard and blessing.

THE MID-ATLANTIC RIDGE

Iceland is home to and has been shaped by the primary forces that have molded the entire earth: volcanic eruptions, earthquakes, and erosion. Some scientists believe that these forces are more active on Iceland than in any other country in the world. In fact, Iceland's more than 200 volcanoes have unleashed an estimated one-third of Earth's total output of lava during the past five centuries. On average, one eruption occurs every five years; fortunately, however, such events rarely happen where anyone lives.

The island of Iceland is located on the Mid-Atlantic Ridge, a huge rupture zone on the floor of the Atlantic Ocean. This underwater mountain range is part of a continuous 37,000-mile-long (60,000 kilometers) backbone of Earth that extends from the Arctic Ocean to beyond the southern tip of Africa, and continues on through both the Pacific and Indian Oceans. The ridge marks the "zone of divergence" that comprises the points from which the ocean floors spread. (Most movement of the earth's surface occurs along narrow zones, or boundaries, between the earth's plates. Divergent boundaries are those where new crust is produced as the earth's plates pull away from each other; perhaps the best known of the divergent boundaries is the Mid-Atlantic Ridge.)

The spreading movement in the ocean floor is referred to as sea floor spreading and is a part of the plate tectonic process popularly called "continental drift," in which the positions of landmasses on Earth's surface slowly (about one inch [2.5 centimeters] a year) but constantly change in relation to other landmasses. For example, the North American continent is moving westward from Europe. Africa is moving northward toward Europe. India is moving northward, essentially "crashing" into Asia and in the process creating the towering Himalayas. Sea floor spreading over the past 100 to 200 million years has caused the Atlantic Ocean to grow from a tiny inlet of water between the continents of Europe, Africa, and North and South America into the vast ocean we know today.

From its position straddling the Mid-Atlantic Ridge, the volcanic island of Iceland offers scientists a wonderful natural laboratory for studying on land those processes occurring along the submerged parts of the ridge. Iceland is a product of the continual splitting along the spreading center of the ridge located between the North American and Eurasian Plates. The resulting volcanic eruptions over the past 20 million years or so allowed enough magma to well up and accumulate to form the island country. This makes Iceland a very young country, geologically. It will continue to change, and to experience both volcanic and seismic (earthquake) activity as the plates continue to move very slowly apart.

GLACIERS

As mentioned earlier, Iceland is not really a land buried under vast expanses of ice, as its name suggests. The island's glaciers are not remnants of the Ice Age; rather, they have developed during the past few thousand years. There are five major glaciers, the largest of which is Vatnajökull (*jökull* means "glacier"). This 3,180-square-mile (8,236 square kilometers) ice mass, located in the southeast, covers an area greater than the island's other four glaciers combined. Its ice reaches a thickness of 3,280 feet (1,000 meters) and sits atop an active "hot spot" that creates many volcanoes. The result of this collision of fire and ice is discussed later in this chapter. Of the other four glaciers, Hofsjökull and Langjökull are located in the central part of the island. The much smaller Myrdalsjökull and Eyjafjallajökull are located near the coast in the far south.

SURFACE PHYSICAL FEATURES

The surface physical features of Iceland all have one thing in common—they are of volcanic origin. However, the various regions of Iceland exhibit different types of surface origins. In some areas, land built by volcanic action is most evident. Elsewhere, the results of rock weathering (disintegration) and erosion dominate the landscape.

In southern Iceland, sprawling and contrasting stretches of farmland and wild heaths, lava fields and sands, and mountains and geothermal fields dominate the landscape. Inland rugged highlands tower in sharp contrast to the island's coastal zone and constantly churning sea. Grassy plains, heather-clad moors, and moss-covered lava fields are found on the coastward portion, grading into the mountainous interior. Geysers and other hot springs are found scattered about much of the region.

Eastern Iceland, too, is a land of vast contrasts. A portion of this region is covered by the world's largest lava field, the 1,740-square-mile (4,500 square kilometers) Odadahraun. The Odadahraun bears the closest resemblance of any place on Earth to the surface of the moon. It is desolate, rugged, and was chosen by the U.S. space program as its training ground for the first lunar landings. This bleak and barren area borders, in sharp contrast, plains that not only are important agriculturally, but also contain the largest woodlands in Iceland. Mountains found in this section contain a large number of waterfalls. Herds of reindeer can often be seen roaming across the grassy heaths.

In northern Iceland, contrasting forces of fire and ice have combined to shape the landscape. This area contains some of the world's largest lava fields. Some of the region is covered with plants and mosses, but much of the surface here is barren of plant life. A number of volcanoes and erupting fissures are

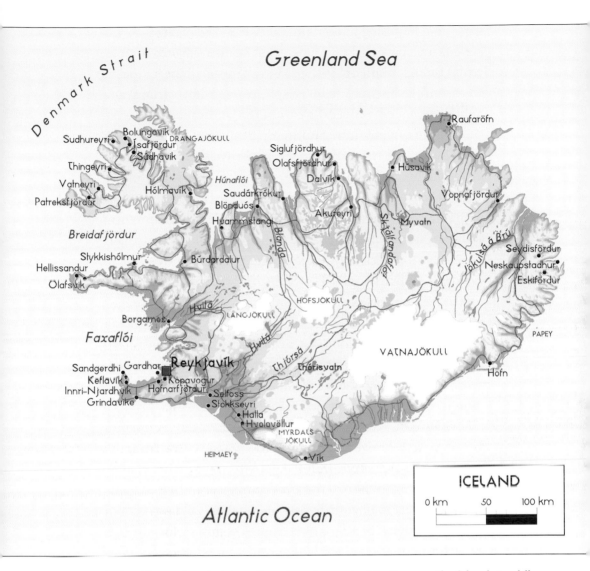

Denmark Strait

Greenland Sea

Sudhureyri
Bolungavik
Ísafjördur
Súdavik
DRANGAJÖKULL
Thingeyri
Vatneyri
Patreksfjördur
Hólmavík
Siglufjördhur
Olafsfjördhur
Dalvík
Húsavik
Raufaröfn
Vopnafjördur
Húnaflói
Saudárkrókur
Blönduós
Hvammstangi
Akureyri
Myvatn
Breidafjördur
Stykkishólmur
Hellissandur
Olafsvik
Búrdardalur
Jökulsá á Brú
Seydisfördur
Neskaupstadhur
Eskifördur
HOFSJÖKULL
Hvítá
LANGJÖKULL
Borgarnes
Hvítá
Faxaflói
Thjórsá
VATNAJÖKULL
PAPEY
Sandgerdhi
Gardhar
Reykjavik
Keflavík
Kopavogur
Innri-Njardhvik
Hafnarfjördur
Grindavike
Selfoss
Stokkseyri
Halla
Hvolovöllur
Thórisvatn
Hofn
MYRDALS-JÖKULL
HEIMAEY
Vík

Atlantic Ocean

ICELAND

0 km   50   100 km

Iceland is a uniquely interesting place for geologists. Because the island straddles the underwater Mid-Atlantic Ridge, scientists are able to study the ways in which the plates of the earth's crust shift over time. Iceland also provides scientists with a theater of volcanic activity, both ancient and ongoing.

still very active here, and recently formed craters can be seen in many places.

Western Iceland, like the country's other physical regions, offers an endless variety of contrasting landscapes. There are dark and imposing mountains and tree-clad valleys; fertile agricultural pastures and moss and heather-covered moors; gentle brooks, impressive waterfalls, and rushing rivers. Marshlands and geothermal fields with steaming hot springs and bubbling mud pots are also a part of the landscape of the west.

The final region, the Southwest Peninsula, is the island's most important. It is home to the majority of the population, including the capital and largest city, Reykjavik. Much of the area is lava-covered, testifying to violent past eruptions. While such lava can appear in a variety of forms—some ropy in form and quite smooth, others so sharp and jagged that it is virtually impossible to walk across them without cutting one's shoes to shreds—in this area of Iceland, large areas of the lava fields are covered with moss, since no eruption has taken place here for several hundred years.

The Blue Lagoon, located at Svartsengi in southwestern Iceland, is perhaps the world's largest hot tub. Located in the middle of a huge lava field, the large pool was formed by the runoff from a power plant that uses geothermal heat to produce electricity and fresh hot water from seawater. The lagoon measures several hundred feet in length and several hundred feet wide. Water running into the pool from the power plant is rich in silica and other elements. The silica selectively absorbs incoming solar radiation, reflecting the blue of the sky and resulting in the pool's dark blue color. The silica mud also has covered the rough lava at the bottom of the pool, giving it a very lumpy but smooth surface. The water is believed to have powers for healing skin and other ailments and is used by many people for health reasons. Of course, most people simply enjoy a soak in a very unique setting.

Volcanic action has created a variety of other features. Cinder cones, for example, dot the landscape in many areas. These conical hills are built up as eruptions hurl volcanic ash, cinders, and other solid objects into the air. As they fall back to earth, the materials accumulate in a classic cone-shaped heap,

Located in southwestern Iceland, the Blue Lagoon could be called the world's largest hot tub. Fed by runoff from a nearby power plant, the lagoon's waters are rich in silica, which causes the water to reflect its deep blue color. The natural geothermal heat of the lagoon provides a healing warmth to Icelandic bathers.

with a characteristic crater at the top. Another unique feature associated with some lava flows is the columnar jointing that occurs as the molten rock cools, contracts, and solidifies. This results in the formation of basalt columns that are often exposed at the surface through erosion.

Much of Iceland's coast is rugged. In some places, vertical cliffs plunge directly into the sea. Numerous sea arches, sea caves, and sea stacks (chimney-like rocks sticking out of the water) add to the coastal region's spectacular scenery.

Waterfalls are found virtually all over the island. They are formed as snow and glacial meltwaters cascade down Iceland's many cliff faces, which were created by lava flows or, in some cases, by geologic faulting.

EARTHQUAKES

Earthquakes frequently occur along fault lines. In fact, seismic activity (earth tremors) and volcanic activity often are located in the same area, since both owe their existence to plate tectonics. Since Iceland lies astride the Mid-Atlantic Ridge, the island experiences both environmental hazards. In fact, it one of Earth's most seismically active spots. Hundreds of quakes occur each year, but few are damaging. Of the several hundred "major" quakes to strike Iceland during recent centuries, few were greater than 5.0 in magnitude. The fact that they occur on a regular basis keeps stress from building up in the moving rock. The tremors, therefore, occur in many gentle earth movements rather than in fewer but much sharper and damaging jolts of movement.

MAJOR VOLCANIC ERUPTIONS

Iceland experiences repeated volcanic eruptions, an average of one every five years. Several, however, stand out as major events: the Mount Laki eruption of 1783–1784, the formation of Surtsey Island in 1963–1967, and the eruption beneath Vatnajökull in 1996.

The Laki Eruptions, 1783–1784

In the spring of 1783, lava began to flow from a huge fissure located just to the west of Vatnajökull. This volcanic event, known as the Laki eruptions (named after a volcano in the area), proved to be devastating—the most destructive natural disaster in the island's history. For nearly a year, explosion after explosion occurred from the 140 craters located along the 20-mile (32 meters) crack in the earth's crust. Lava flow buried an area of nearly 220 square miles (570 square kilometers), making it the world's largest lava field resulting from a single series of eruptions. As a result of the eruptions, the area offers some of Iceland's most spectacular scenery.

The event was described by a witness, the Reverend Jon Stingrimsson, in his book, *Fires of the Earth:*

> [The eruptions] began with the earth heaving upwards with a great screaming noise of wind from its depths, then splitting asunder, ripping and tearing, as if a crazed animal [was] tearing something apart. Flames . . . soon stretched upwards from each [volcanic crater]. Great slabs of rock . . . were cast up indescribably high into the air, backwards and forwards, with great crashes, flares of fire and spouts of sand, smoke, and fumes. Oh, how fearsome it was to look [upon this awesome event].

It is estimated that one-fourth of the population at the time, some 10,000 people, died as a result of inhaling poisonous gases emitted during the eruptions, or from starvation. Three-fourths of the island's livestock also died, directly or indirectly, as a result of the eruptions, and an atmospheric blanket of haze spread around the Northern Hemisphere, cooling temperatures. In the eastern United States, the winter temperature was nearly 15°F (5°C) colder than the 225-year average.

Birth of an Island, 1963–1967

From 1963 to 1967, Iceland and much of the world watched as new land—the island of Surtsey—was born and rose from the sea. This 1-square-mile, 555-foot-high (2.6 square kilometers, 169 meters) volcanic island is centered at 63°18′ north latitude and 20°36′ west longitude, or about 25 miles (40 kilometers) off the southwest coast of Iceland. It was named Surtsey for Surtur, the fire-possessing giant of Norse mythology. The relatively recent creation of this new island reminds us that volcanic activity and land building is still taking place on and around Iceland. Since Surtsey stopped growing in 1967, powerful ocean waves and howling winds have eroded a third of its mass away.

The island is of great scientific value. Biologists have been

Icelanders live each day with the threat of volcanic activity beneath their feet. In the autumn of 1996, a dramatic eruption beneath an Icelandic glacier resulted in a massive ice melt and flood. Although no lives were lost, the flood wiped out the bridge span that served as the main roadway connection between the eastern and western portions of the country.

given a wonderful opportunity to study not only the method of its formation but also how a new, sterile environment is colonized by plant and animal life.

Volcanic Eruption Beneath Vatnajökull, 1996

In November 1996, the eruption of a volcano under Vatnajö-kull caused great quantities of ice to melt on the underside of the ice cap. This huge pool of water finally broke free from the south end of the glacier, causing a catastrophic flood. Maximum flood rates reached 1.6 million cubic feet (45,310 cubic meters) per second (about 12 million gallons, or 45 million liters). This torrential type of flood, called a *jökulhlaup* by Icelanders, is now also known by this name by the rest of the world. When the rising waters issued from the edge of the glacier, lumps of ice 30 feet (10 meters) high and weighing a thousand tons were carried along. This water poured across a stretch of glacially deposited sand and ultimately into the sea. Fortunately, this area is not permanently inhabited, so no loss of life occurred. However, the rushing floodwater washed out several miles of highway, electrical power transmission cables, and a several mile long bridge. The bridge was built to handle the normal periodic flooding, but the volume of water in November 1996 was too great. Thus, the flood effectively cut links between the eastern and western part of Iceland, isolating the regions from one another. The two areas are connected with a road that follows the northern coast, but this route is much longer and is difficult to travel in the winter.

WEATHER AND CLIMATE

Iceland enjoys a much milder climate than its name and location close to the Arctic Circle would imply. The overall air temperatures are at least 9°F (4°C) warmer than would be expected at this latitude. The reason: a branch of the Gulf Stream — also known as the North Atlantic Drift, a broad current or "river" of warm water from the equatorial region — flows along the island's southern and western coast. This greatly moderates the climate and explains why Iceland is so much warmer than Greenland, which does not lie in the path of a warm current. In some respects, however, the current is a mixed blessing. When the mild Atlantic air comes in contact with colder Arctic air, the result is frequent changes in weather and many storms. This is particularly true during the winter months, when differences in temperature between the two air masses are greatest.

The clash of air masses contributes to higher levels of precipitation in the southern and western parts of the island than in the north. Frequent high winds are also a normal condition, resulting from the contrast in air and water temperatures. The average temperature in the lowlands near the southern coast is about 54°F (12°C) in July and a relatively balmy 30°F (-1°C) in January. Although Iceland lies at the same latitude as Fairbanks, Alaska, its winter temperatures are comparable to those of Kansas or Massachusetts. Nonetheless, the winter season is one of long nights and severe winter storms. Snow is common from around the beginning of November until the middle of April, particularly in the northern region.

Perhaps the most difficult aspect of the Icelandic winter for many people to become accustomed to is its very short periods of daylight and long periods of darkness, a condition that reflects Iceland's high latitude. (Just the opposite conditions—long days and short nights—are experienced during the summer). In late December, the sun barely peeks above the southern horizon, and within an hour it is gone.

Summer in Iceland lasts from late May to early September. During the first half of this season, the sun appears above the horizon for almost 24 hours a day, while the period of darkness is very short or, in the north, nonexistent. However, even during the middle of summer when the daylight period is longer, the sky is frequently cloudy or overcast and the sunshine does not warm the air much. Thus, during the daytime, the air is usually cool and nighttime temperatures are often quite cold.

Throughout the year, the air in Iceland is damp, thereby intensifying the cold. Moist air moving onto land from the Atlantic Ocean brings about this humid condition, which makes both summer and winter climates less comfortable than temperature alone would indicate.

On the high lava plateau regions of the interior and the north, winter conditions can be encountered any time of the year. Here, blizzards are not uncommon during the summer season, and certainly occur frequently during the long winter season. Along the highways of the northern interior, bright orange-colored survival huts are frequently seen. About 10 by

12 feet (3 to 3.7 meters) in size, these buildings are equipped with bunks, emergency food supplies, first-aid kits, and radios. They are not locked and are to be used by travelers who are stranded by year-round stormy conditions.

PLANT AND ANIMAL LIFE

About 540 different species of plants can be found growing wild in Iceland. Large areas of vegetated ground are marshy, or are covered by various species of moss. In the north, a tundra ecosystem dominates, with its various species of mosses, lichens, and sedges. Vegetation includes some 500 species of low-growing shrubs. Bearberry, crowberry, dwarf birch, heather, and willow are the most common species.

Mosses and lichen cover the surface of many of the lower elevation lava fields. Greenhouses, heated with geothermal water, are used extensively for growing many kinds of vegetables, flowers, and other plants in a protected environment. In fact, much of Iceland's produce, including peppers, tomatoes, and cucumbers, are grown under these conditions.

Today, Iceland is essentially treeless. Several thousand years ago, however, most of the island was covered with lush forest. Ancient Icelandic writings from the twelfth century tell how, three centuries earlier (in the 800s), the first settlers found a country that was covered with trees from mountain to shore. Over the centuries, the once dense woodlands were chopped down for timber and firewood. Grazing sheep also took their toll, as did harsh winters and areas of volcanic ash that prevented trees from taking root. Extensive reforestation work began in the early twentieth century. Although there is only one true forest in the country, Iceland plants more trees per person than any other nation in the world (16 trees for every man, woman, and child!).

Driftwood is a blessing in an almost treeless country, and Iceland's shoreline has an abundance of this resource. In the past, much of the driftwood was used for building. Today it is used primarily for fence posts. Along many of the coastlines and beaches, it is a common sight to see large tree trunks that have drifted with ocean currents primarily from Europe and North America.

There are some 75 nesting species of birds in the country, many in very large numbers. Huge colonies of puffins, guille-mots, gannets, and many different species of other waterfowl make Iceland a bird-watcher's paradise. The king of Icelandic birds is the magnificent sea eagle, while the common eider duck provides a valuable product—eiderdown—to supplement farmers' incomes. This soft down is collected from the female ducks' nests after the babies have hatched and grown up. The Icelanders use it to make down-filled comforters, vests, and other clothing items. The majority of the eiderdown collected is exported.

Several species of gulls, ravens, shovelers, snow buntings, starlings, and wrens are residents of Iceland, along with the common house sparrow, redwing, and swallow. Many of these are summertime residents, migrating to warmer portions of the world during the winter season.

Iceland has only a single native land mammal, the Arctic fox. Four other species of land animals currently found in the country are the mouse, rat, mink, and reindeer (imported from Norway in the eighteenth century). The mink are descendents of animals that escaped from fur farms in the 1930s. The mouse and rat found their way onto Iceland from ships docked in the various ports.

Contrary to expectation, there are no polar bears or walruses in Iceland. On rare occasion, a polar bear will float on an ice floe from Greenland to Iceland, but it does not remain a permanent resident.

Fish of many kinds are abundant both in freshwater streams and lakes and in Iceland's coastal waters. Some 40,000–60,000 seals breed along the coastline, and there are tens of thousands of whales within Iceland's territorial waters. For decades a limited number of whales were caught each year,

Iceland is home to a variety of interesting plants and animals, including many sea birds like these puffins. Puffins are excellent divers and rely on a diet of eel, smelt, and other small fish for survival. Iceland's 75 nesting species of birds have made it a sought-after location for bird-watching.

for both domestic use and export. Today, Iceland no longer hunts whales. In recent years, the number of whales has been decreasing to the point that some species are endangered and threatened with extinction.

THE SEA

Although volcanoes and glaciers dominate its landforms, Iceland has always focused on the sea. The island's weather and climate is more influenced by Atlantic waters than by latitudinal location. Temperatures are strongly moderated by the warm waters of the North Atlantic Drift, which also cause Iceland to receive considerably more precipitation than most other locations at the same latitude. Water evaporated from the relatively warm sea falls over land in the form of rain or snow,

The volcanic activity below Iceland generates a great deal of geothermal energy. When heat generated by volcanic activity meets with Iceland's chilly waters, the result is often a hot spring, like the one shown here. Geothermal heat is also used to heat 80 percent of Iceland's homes, without the need of a furnace.

At present, approximately 1,500 megawatts (MW, a million watts) of geothermal energy have been harnessed in Iceland. The main energy supplies (except imported oil and gasoline for various types of engines) are derived from hydroelectric power plants, which include an overall system of 14 large dams. Electrical generation from steam (geothermal) driven turbines also contributes greatly to the total electricity produced.

Hot-spring and geyser locations can change, disappear, or be created due to tectonic and volcanic activity. The fissures extending upward from the underground magma chambers can be closed or opened. Hot springs also change their appearance depending on the amount of precipitation that occurs over time.

Iceland has no minerals worth extracting, no economic coal deposits, and no known gas or oil fields. Its subsurface is rich in low-grade iron and titanium, but these metals are not worth mining. However, Iceland's volcanoes have been generous in providing important natural resources for Iceland's population. Scoria, a porous lava rock, is used for road building and foundations; pumice is used in making lightweight concrete or plates; and rock wool is made from remelted basalt. Iceland is self-sufficient in the production of cement for concrete. Salt is produced from geothermal brine. Even freshwater shells are used; they are turned into silica powder by oven-drying, the heat for which comes from geothermal energy.

Iceland's natural environment and its resultant landscapes—molded by fire and ice and surrounded by the sea—play an essential role in nearly every aspect of Icelanders' lives. From its fish come food and oil, from geothermal energy comes heat, and from the country's rapidly flowing streams comes more than 95 percent of its electricity. Natural hazards—such as frequent earthquakes, violent volcanic eruptions, blinding blizzards, and torrential floods—serve as reminders that Icelanders are never far-removed from nature. In the following chapters, you too will often be reminded of their importance as you learn more about the country's history, its people, and their varied activities.

While ancient Greek, Phoenician, and Roman explorers may have first reached Iceland over two thousand years ago, the land is most often associated with the Vikings. In the year 874, a Norseman named Ingolfur Arnarson became Iceland's first permanent settler. This ship sculpture pays homage to Iceland's Viking roots.

3

Iceland
Through Time

I n this chapter, our primary focus is on Iceland's culture
   as created by its people and their past. The country has a
   fascinating and somewhat contradictory history. Among
major world nations, for example, it was one of the very last
countries to be settled. In this respect, it has a very brief history,
although its governing body is one of the oldest in the world. In
this chapter, you will find answers to questions such as: Who are
the Icelanders? From where and when did they come? What has
happened on this small island since their arrival? How have they
forged a way of life in this harsh and remote place that in many
respects has come to be one of the world's best places to live?
How do they govern themselves? Our trip through time begins
in northern mists.

NORTHERN MISTS AND MYSTERY

Dense fog and mist shrouds the northern Atlantic Ocean much of the time. Howling winds and towering waves, piercing rain and sleet, huge icebergs and floating sea ice are common-place. During the long winter months, the sun barely peeks above the horizon and visibility is limited to a few short hours. These are just some of the conditions that make navigation treacherous in the seas around Iceland.

Just as northern mist limits visibility, some aspects of Iceland's early history also are shrouded in mystery. Some historical geographers believe that Mediterranean Europeans may have reached Iceland at least four centuries before the dawn of the Christian era. Early Phoenician sailors told of seas that would hold ships in place (sea ice?), where monsters rose above the water (whales?), and where darkness fell over the earth (northern latitudes?). There is no evidence, however, that these Phoenicians actually reached Iceland.

To the ancient Greeks, the place called *Thule* was believed to be the northernmost area of the inhabitable world. They had learned of this northern land from the travels of a Greek explorer, Pytheas, who, in about 330 B.C., had sailed northward from the Mediterranean. It is certain that he sailed around the islands of Great Britain, which he described in considerable detail. While there, he was told of an island called Thule located six sailing days north of Britain. Pytheas continued his voyage northward and reached the place that he described as being the outermost of all inhabited lands and a place where the sun went to sleep [early]. The Greek geographer Strabo, writing around the time of Christ, said of Pytheas's trip:

> Pytheas . . . speaks of the waters around Thule and of those places where land properly speaking no longer exists, nor sea nor air, but a mixture of these things, like a "marine lung," . . . on which one can neither walk nor sail.

The marine lung that Strabo described, "on which one can neither walk nor sail," almost certainly was thick sea ice rising and falling as waves passed beneath. In northern mists, sea, land, and sky often blend into one imperceptible landscape in which it is impossible to distinguish one from the other. Is this a description of the sea around Iceland? Was Pytheas the first person to reach this remote island that is frequently shrouded in fog? Unfortunately, we will never know. But the name "Thule" was used in reference to Iceland for some time during the Middle Ages.

It appears that even the Romans may have ventured into the waters of the North Atlantic soon after the dawn of the Christian era. Roman coins, dating from before 300 A.D., have been found in several locations in Iceland. Whether they were left behind by Roman sailors, or brought by early Nordic settlers, remains in doubt. The coins' origin remains a mystery, and there is no other evidence linking early Romans to Iceland and the region of northern mists.

SECLUSION FOUND AND LOST

Irish monks, seeking a remote location where they could serve God in total seclusion, were the first known settlers of Iceland. The exact date of their arrival remains open to question. Ancient Celtic (Irish) ruins recently discovered and excavated by archaeologists have been dated to about 680 A.D. Historical writings suggest that the monks reached the island early in the eighth century. Other writings indicate that they were established on a remote island that they called "Thule" by the mid-700s. The Irish monk Decuil wrote that other monks had been to Thule around 795. He reported that during midsummer there was bright light during both day and night—so bright, in fact, that the monks could pick lice from their shirts even in the middle of the night.

Regardless of when the monks arrived, several things are known about their time on Thule. First, they did not establish a permanent settlement, so they made no long-term impact on the island. Second, a small colony of monks was still living there when Norse (Viking) explorers first arrived in around 800. An early history mentions that when the Vikings reached Iceland, they met people whom they called *papar*, or fathers. It is also known that soon after the Norsemen settled Iceland, the monks vanished. Why they left the island is not known. Perhaps they simply found that the solitude they had sought on Iceland had been broken by the newly arrived "heathens" from Scandinavia.

VIKING EXPANSION

The Vikings came from Norway, Sweden, and Denmark. From the eighth to the eleventh centuries they were perhaps the world's foremost explorers, colonizers, warriors, and traders. To these brave seafarers, Iceland was just a short, seven- or eight-day voyage away. They became the island's first permanent settlers, thereby establishing a Scandinavian cultural imprint that remains dominant in Iceland today. It was not until 1944 that Iceland was able to free itself from more than 1,000 years of Scandinavian political control.

In 874, a Norseman named Ingolfur Arnarson became Iceland's first permanent settler when he built a home on a calm *vik*, or bay. Because the steam from the area's many hot springs looked like smoke to Arnarson, he called his new place Reykjavik, or Bay of Smoke. Today, of course, the country's capital and largest city now occupies the site on which he settled.

The next fifty years, from the mid-870s to about 930, are known as the Age of Settlement. During this half-century period, the island was flooded with new settlers from Scandinavia. The names of more than 400 settlers are recorded in the ancient *Book of Icelanders* and *Book of Settlements*. These two histories list settlers' names and family backgrounds and identify the places from which they came and where they settled down. But the books only listed the names of important leaders; hundreds of others flocked to the island in search of land and opportunity. Most came from Norway, but Sweden and Denmark also contributed to the wave. Others arrived from the British Isles, particularly Ireland and Scotland, and from the many small islands surrounding northern Great Britain. By 930 nearly all the good coastal land was claimed and occupied. It is estimated that some 60,000 people lived on the island at that time—nearly a quarter of the number living there today. The base population, racial stock, and cultural foundation that would characterize Iceland more than a thousand years later were now in place.

Early Trade

For all but a few commodities—such as fish, mutton, and wool—these early Icelanders were totally dependent on shipping. In the stormy north Atlantic, however, sailing was hazardous and ships often were damaged or lost. With few trees and no iron available on the island to repair the ships, import of lumber and iron was essential. In addition, grain and flour were major imports of the time. In exchange, Iceland's exports included dried fish, wool, and cloth.

FORMATION OF A COMMONWEALTH

Iceland's early settlers often came as groups from various locations. Once in Iceland, each group settled in its own territory and one leader rose to govern "his" people, establishing rules by which they would live and worship. In return for his "services," the people paid taxes. This system created a small number of rich and powerful leaders who governed in a number of settlements scattered primarily about the country's coastal area.

This pattern of settlement and control led to unrest, lawlessness, and periodic open conflict among groups. While leaders quarreled among themselves, seeking greater power, most people wanted to live peaceful lives. Some leaders believed that the entire island should be brought under one set of laws and that all the island's people should be unified as one society. It was this early vision that led to the world's first parliamentary government and to the unification of what today is a single country.

Parliament (the *Althing*)

After Icelanders agreed to unite, they needed to decide upon the laws by which they would be governed. Around 920, one of their leaders was sent to Norway to study its laws and government. After three years, he returned with many ideas. Soon a code of law was recommended for the island, and, in the town of Thingvellir just north of Thingvallavatn, a lake east of Reykjavik, a parliament assembled in 930. This parliament, called the Althing, marked the first time an entire country was ruled by a single national assembly. Iceland became a commonwealth, and the Althing is believed to be the world's oldest existing legislative body.

Iceland's formal government began as a democracy, and the tradition continues today, more than a thousand years later. From the beginning, not only did chieftains and other rich and powerful persons attend the Althing sessions, but people from all walks of life came from throughout the country to attend the annual gathering. In fact, it became somewhat of a national annual festival. Historian Jon R. Hjalmarsson described the assembly as "a true melting pot for culture, national feeling and unity."

The early government had no president or king. No military or police force was established. A speaker was elected to a three-year term, but he had no power to enforce laws. Rather, the person holding this office had to memorize and be able to recite all the laws since they were not written down until 1117.

AGE OF EXPLORATION AND SAGAS

The period between 930 and about 1030 was a time of heroic events. It was the century best remembered and described in the famous Icelandic sagas. These stories and poems were

Iceland is home to the world's oldest surviving governing body. Its Parliament (called the Althing) was established around 930 A.D. in the town of Thingvellir. Today the site is part of a National Park.

written mostly during the twelfth and thirteenth centuries from oral histories that had been passed down from generation to generation.

Westward to Greenland

For the brave and skilled sailors from Iceland, it was just a matter of time before they would reach Greenland and lands still farther to the west. Less than 200 miles (320 kilometers) west of Iceland, Greenland was first reached sometime during the mid–tenth century. Soon thereafter, in 980, Erik the Red, the Norwegian explorer, settled there and named the ice-buried island Greenland, hoping that the attractive name would draw more settlers from tree-barren Iceland. He was soon joined by his son Leifur, or Leif Ericsson.

On to Vinland (America)

Sometime before 1000, an Icelander named Bjarni Herjolfsson sailed westward from Iceland in hopes of reaching the growing Greenland colony. Losing his way, he sailed much further south, where he saw a large and unfamiliar land. Rather than investigating, he turned back and finally reached Greenland. Here, Leif Ericsson heard about this new land lying to the west and decided to seek it out himself. In about 1000, with a crew of thirty-five, he set sail. Little did he know what lay ahead!

Leif Ericsson's party first reached a rocky place that they named Helluland (believed to be what is now Baffin Island, off far-northeastern Canada). Sailing southward for several days, they reached a wooded land they called Markland (coastal Labrador). Still farther south, they reached a coast where vines resembling grapes grew on the shores; they called this place Vinland. The location of Vinland was long debated, but in 1960 stone ruins were discovered and excavated at L'Anse aux Meadows, a site at the northern tip of the island of Newfoundland, that were determined to be those of a 1,000-year-old Viking settlement. Icelandic Vikings thus were the first known European discoverers of what is now America.

ACCEPTANCE OF CHRISTIANITY

While Christian monks were the first visitors to Iceland, and many of the early settlers, particularly those from Ireland, were devout in Christian faith, many Icelanders held "pagan" beliefs. The first known Christian missionary to reach Iceland

In about 1000 A.D., Leif Eriksson sailed west in search of a land seen but not visited by another Icelandic explorer. Sailing southwest, he reached a place he called Vinland, at what is now the northern tip of Newfoundland in Canada. The statue shown here commemorates Eriksson's journey.

began his work in 981, and within 20 years, many Icelanders had adopted the Christian faith. After a period of heated debates between Christians and followers of pagan beliefs, the Christians prevailed, and the Althing adopted Catholicism as the country's official religion. All Icelanders were required to join the faith, and for more than 500 years, the Catholic Church was Iceland's most powerful institution, serving as a political, as well as religious, influence. The Church also helped broaden Icelandic culture and expand the islanders' intellectual horizons, since

Icelanders who traveled to Europe to train to become clergy brought back with them European ways of thinking and living.

CENTURIES OF HARDSHIP

The period between the dawn of the eleventh century and the early nineteenth century was a troubled time for Iceland. In 1104, the volcano Mt. Hekla erupted, burying nearly half the country under as much as three feet (1 meter) of volcanic ash and other debris.

The thirteenth century was a particularly difficult period. Much of the natural environment was in ruin. Iceland still had not fully recovered from the Hekla eruption. Woodlands had been cleared and there was little lumber for building or repairing boats. Sheep had overgrazed much of the island, resulting in severe soil erosion. Politically, the country was also in turmoil. A small number of wealthy families held much of the land and power. Eventually, in 1262, weakened by internal conflict, Icelanders gave up their independence. In order to bring hoped-for peace, rule of the island nation was handed to the king of Norway (and later the king of Denmark). Foreign rule in Iceland was to last for 682 years.

Norwegian king Magnus (who became known as Magnus the Reformer) was concerned about the lawlessness of the Icelandic people. He believed that the country needed a new set of laws. In 1271, for the first time in Iceland's history, a book of laws was published. These new legal codes did not gain full support of Icelanders, however, and they were revised and republished in 1280. The new codes were more widely accepted and remained in effect for centuries.

The 1300s were a period of much change, not always for the better. This was particularly true of the island's cultural life. The Great Plague (also called the Black Death) was sweeping much of Europe and much of Norway. As a result, shipping and trade links between Norway and Iceland declined sharply. Another eruption of Mt. Hekla once again devastated a huge

During the 1400s, Iceland suffered a devastating plague that killed nearly half of the small nation's population. This illustration shows the mass burials resulting from the plague.

area of the island. Famine stalked the land, resulting in many deaths. The writing of the classic sagas declined, as did other forms of literature. Conflict was also growing between the king of Norway and the Church. Iceland became immersed in its own Dark Age.

Severe hardship also marked Icelandic life in the fifteenth century (1400s), during which the island was twice ravaged by the Great Plague. It is estimated that as much as one-half of the population—rich and poor, powerful and powerless alike—died. Farms were abandoned and fishing declined.

The cycle of misfortune continued during the sixteenth

and seventeenth centuries. Natural disasters once again stalked the land as the conflicting agents of fire and ice ravaged the island. In 1783–1784, Iceland experienced what proved to be its greatest natural catastrophe—the Laki eruptions. At the same time, a severe earthquake destroyed many farms in southern Iceland. The combined events resulted in the deaths of an estimated three-quarters of the island's livestock and one-quarter of its human population. Also, during a period extending from the thirteenth to nineteenth centuries, much of the Northern Hemisphere was plunged into a period of bitter cold (known to meteorologists as "The Little Ice Age"). On Iceland, crops failed, resulting in the starvation of thousands of people and livestock. By the mid-1800s, Iceland had experienced nearly 1,000 years of severe hardship.

THE PROTESTANT REFORMATION

During its centuries of hardship, life became much more difficult for the Icelandic people. It was a period of repeated environmental catastrophe, disease, and famine. It also was a period of cultural decline. Economic, social, and political conditions suffered, as did the people. One event, however, did have a profound impact on Icelandic culture—the Protestant Reformation.

By the mid–sixteenth century, Catholicism had established a 500-year hold on Iceland's people and religious landscape. But this was soon to change, in a major transformation of the island's religious culture. In 1517, a German, Martin Luther, began a formal protest in Germany against what he believed to be abuses in the established Catholic Church. His move toward reform resulted in a break among his followers from Catholicism. The new religion they formed as a result what became called the Protestant Reformation bears his name—Lutheran.

In 1537, the Danish king—who, in 1380, had taken control of both Norway and Iceland—adopted the Lutheran faith. A year later, he attempted to establish the Lutheran religion in Iceland. By 1540, the New Testament had been translated into Icelandic, thereby becoming the first book ever written in the Icelandic language. In 1541, Lutheranism was adopted by the Althing as the country's official faith.

Many Icelanders did not welcome the new religion, which was much different than Catholicism. Lutheranism, after all, had been imposed by force, and many practices with which the people had long been accustomed were now prohibited. All things Catholic—including buildings, worship, clergy, art, saints—were destroyed, forbidden, or driven out. To many people, the change came as a terrible culture shock. Religious beliefs, after all, are at the very foundation of many cultures.

Today, Iceland recognizes freedom of religion, and many faiths are represented within the island's population. The church no longer plays as important a role as it did in times past. The Evangelical Lutheran faith, however, remains Iceland's official state church, in which some 93 percent of all Icelanders claim membership. Iceland's president is the leading church authority and ministers are government employees. Lutheranism has continued to be a strong influence on Icelandic culture.

HOME RULE AND INDEPENDENCE

By the mid–nineteenth century, Icelanders were becoming tired of foreign rule. The island was emerging from nearly a millennium of hardship and the people looked to the future with optimism. The economy was improving. In 1843, the Althing was reinstated as a consulting body, although Denmark retained the right to veto decisions. By 1854, Iceland became free to trade with all countries, thereby ending several centuries of economic oppression. In 1874, the 1,000th anniversary of Iceland's first permanent settlement, a huge step was taken toward independence: the country adopted its own constitution and gained control of its own finances.

Iceland was not always a free nation. Ruled for years by Denmark, the country was officially recognized by the Danes in 1919, though the Danish King remained head of state. It was not until June 17, 1944 that Svenin Bjornsson (shown here) was elected as the country's first president.

Full independence was yet to come, however. Fully thirty years after adopting its own constitution, Iceland was finally granted home rule by the Danes. This gave the country its own government, but with continuing strong ties to Denmark. In 1919, Denmark recognized Iceland as an independent nation, although the Danish king remained the Icelandic head of state. Finally, on June 17, 1944, Iceland declared itself a free and independent republic. Sveinn Bjornsson was elected the country's first president and a new constitution was adopted.

Since gaining its independence, Iceland has prospered. The country has earned a respected place on the stage of world nations. Its people, too, have prospered. In the following chapter, you will learn more about these hardy people and their way of life.

Icelanders take great pride in their national history and culture. Home to just over a quarter million people, Iceland celebrates the anniversary of its independence with a holiday parade featuring costumed marchers.

4

Iceland's People and Their Way of Life

I celanders enjoy one of the world's highest standards of living and longest life expectancies. As has been mentioned, it is one of the world's most literate societies, with nearly 100 percent of all adults able to read and write. Surveys suggest that it is also one of the most honest countries, with very little crime or corruption. In this chapter, you will learn what makes this so.

ICELAND'S PEOPLE

With a population of 286,250 (January 1, 2002, official figure), Iceland has only about half as many people than the least populated U.S. state, Wyoming. The country's population density of seven people per square mile (four per square kilometer) may suggest that people are scattered throughout the island, but this is not the case. Icelandic settlement (where people live) clings to the island's coasts. Nearly all of the country's rugged, partially ice-covered interior is wasteland in terms of economic use, transportation access, and human settlement. Approximately 170,000 people, or nearly 60 percent of the total population, are tightly clustered in and around the capital city, Reykjavik. In fact, nearly all Icelanders are urban— 99 percent of them live in cities or towns with 200 or more people.

Demographically (statistics on the human population), Iceland is a very stable country. Its rate of natural population increase (number of births over deaths) is a relatively low 0.5 percent per year, about the same as that of the United States and well below the world average of 1.3 percent. This small gain is nearly balanced, however, by out-migration, or number of people leaving the island. During recent decades, the country has experienced a very slow and relatively small increase in population.

Living standards and life expectancy go hand in hand. Iceland's people enjoy excellent medical care, are well-educated, and earn good incomes. Under these conditions, most people can expect to have long, healthy, and productive lives. In only four other countries can people expect to live longer than do the residents of Iceland. At birth, Icelanders can expect to live an average of 80 years, with women living to 82 and men to 78, on average.

Iceland also has one of the world's most homogeneous populations. Nearly all of the island's residents can trace their ancestry to Norse (Scandinavian) or Celtic (Irish) roots. As is true of most Nordic peoples, Icelanders tend to have fair skin and blond to light-brown hair. Their culture, or way of life, also tends to be very homogeneous. Nearly everyone lives, worships, dresses, eats, and thinks the same. There is little racial or cultural diversity within the Icelandic population.

LANGUAGE

Icelandic is the country's official language, but most citizens are multilingual, speaking two or more languages. Both Danish and English are taught in the schools and are widely spoken and understood. Many people also speak Norwegian or other European tongues.

Icelandic is a language virtually identical to that spoken by the islanders' Norse forefathers and is nearly unchanged from that spoken by the Vikings more than 1,000 years ago. During the eighth to tenth centuries, all Norse people spoke the same language. Through time, however, each Scandinavian country developed its own tongue—Norwegian, Swedish, and Danish. But Iceland retained the ancient language that has remained virtually unchanged through the centuries. It is, in fact, the oldest modern European language.

One can experience this historic language through the country's legendary "sagas" (meaning "something said"). Beginning in the Middle Ages and continuing on for centuries, Norse stories of feuds, romance, legends, and other events in the lives of the people were passed from generation to generation as oral histories. During the eleventh century, and on through the fourteenth century, writers recorded the sagas. Their writings preserved this valuable history of Icelandic legend, mythology, and other Norse events.

Today, many people are afraid that their language is threatened by change. They are particularly worried about the many new words being introduced through the media and by other means, particularly in response to the appearance of new technologies such as the computer. So concerned are they that an Icelandic Language Committee has been formed to invent words that will keep their language current while still retaining its character. The committee's word for television, for example, is *sjonvarp*, meaning "a throwing out of pictures."

ICELANDIC NAMES

In America, if your name is Jon and your parents are Jim and Mary Larson, your name would be Jon Larson. Larson is your family name, or surname. In Iceland, however, only about 10 percent of Icelanders have surnames. The rest use the system called "patronymics," in which the surname is formed by the father's first name combined with either "son" or "dottir" (daughter). Thus, if Richard and Inga are the children of Jon Stefansson, their names would be Richard Jonsson and Inga Jonsdottir. Because of this system, it is considered proper to address Icelanders by their first names. Also, because there are no "family" names, a woman does not change her name with marriage. Since so many Icelanders have the same name, telephone directories list each person's occupation in addition to his or her name and address.

Many Icelandic toponyms (place names) also indicate the nature of the feature they identify. In chapter 2, for example, you may have noted that the name of the huge glacier Vatnajökull was not followed by the word "glacier." This is because jökull already means glacier. Other similar terms that appear often on the Icelandic map as part of a place name include: *fell* (mountain), *fjordur* (fjord), *floi* (bay), *foss* (falls), *hraun* (lava field), *nes* (peninsula), *vatn* (lake), and *vik* (cove, inlet). By knowing the meaning of such words, the reader will find that maps in fact speak colorfully of the many features they display.

RELIGION

During the mid–sixteenth century, on the heels of the Protestant Reformation, the Lutheran faith became the dominant religion in much of northwestern Europe as well as in Iceland. Today, all Icelanders at birth are registered in the Evangelical Lutheran church, the official state religion; a person must apply to leave church membership. Although religious freedom of choice is practiced, about 93 percent of all Icelanders are registered Lutherans.

Many Icelanders are church members in name only, however. Attendance is often sparse, except for special events such as weddings, baptisms, funerals, and special holiday services. On the other hand, many people are quite devout in their belief in spirits and other supernatural things. According to a survey conducted by the University of Iceland, slightly more than half of all Icelanders believe in elves, "hidden people," and other supernatural notions. It should be remembered, however, that a great many Americans also believe in flying saucers, ghosts, and other strange things!

EDUCATION

In addition to its high rate of literacy, Iceland also boasts the world's highest percentage of school-age youngsters attending school—again, almost 100 percent. All youngsters between the ages of six to sixteen must attend school, and education is free at all levels through university.

The school year varies in length, depending upon location, but most schools are in session for nine months, from the beginning of September through the end of May. One particularly interesting school requirement that seems to be unique to Iceland is that all students must know how to swim in order to graduate from elementary school. This may seem strange, but in a country where so much depends upon the sea and nearly all of the people live near the water, the rule makes very good sense.

Because of the harsh winter weather, many of the schools outside Reykjavik board students. Students live at the school during the week or, in more remote locations, for weeks at a time. During the summer, when schools are not in session, the facilities are used as hotels. Since it is not economically feasible to build hotels that would be filled only during

Iceland boasts one of the highest literacy rates in the world, nearly 100 percent! Icelandic children between the ages of 6 and 16 are required to attend school, and all education from preschool through the university level is free. Even rural schools, like the one shown here, have the latest educational tools.

the short summer tourist season, this arrangement works extremely well. By converting empty schools' sleeping rooms into tourist lodging, the need for hotels is satisfied and money is generated to help support the schools.

Secondary schools are specialized, with curricula divided into three tracks: general education, vocational education, or university preparatory. A high percentage of secondary school graduates continue their education, going on to college or university. The University of Iceland, founded in 1911 and located in Reykjavik, has an enrollment of some 7,000 students and offers undergraduate degrees in more than 20 fields of study. The university also offers advanced degrees in several subjects, but many Icelanders prefer to go abroad to pursue their postgraduate education.

EVERYDAY LIFE

Other than the conditions imposed by its remote location, life in Iceland is not much different than that of Western Europe, or the United States for that matter. The standard of living is one of the world's highest. Incomes are quite high and nearly everyone is in the middle social and economic class; the country has very few extremely wealthy people and extreme poverty is unknown. For most people, life is good.

Cost of Living

Because of its great distance from other lands, the cost of living in Iceland is quite high. Nearly everything must be imported and transportation costs must be added to the prices charged for goods. To help meet family expenses, both husband and wife commonly hold jobs. In fact, nearly 90 percent of all women hold jobs outside the home.

Housing

Housing in Iceland is expensive, yet more than 80 percent of Icelandic families own their own homes or condominiums. Structures must be sturdily built to withstand the frequent earthquakes and howling winds that frequently blow at gale force along the coasts. The most commonly used building material is steel-reinforced concrete. Many houses are painted in pastel colors, perhaps in response to an otherwise somewhat dreary landscape.

Leisure-Time Activities

Icelanders are the world's most avid readers. On a per capita (per person) basis, more books, magazines, and newspapers are published and read in Iceland than in any other country in the world. Reading keeps people occupied during the long, cold, winter nights, and many families take great pride in their personal libraries. The country is home to a number of well-known writers, including Halldor Laxness, who received the Nobel Prize for Literature in 1955.

In addition to the printed media, other forms of communication are very important to Icelanders. The government is anxious to move the country away from its economic dependence on natural resources and toward an "information economy." There are now more than 70 radio stations, 14 television stations, and 7 Internet service providers operating in the country. It has invested heavily in cellular technology and both fiber optic and satellite links to Europe and North America. Today, Iceland has the world's highest rate of mobile phone ownership.

During the short summer, Icelanders enjoy outdoor activities as much as possible. Fishing and hunting are popular, as are hiking, horseback riding, and sailing. Nearly everyone loves to camp, and golf and soccer are popular competitive sports. Winter outdoor activities include skiing, skating, and snowmobiling. Indoors, basketball and handball are popular sports, as are chess and bridge, which help residents pass the long periods of winter darkness. Icelanders can swim throughout the year in both indoor and outdoor pools that are heated by hot springs.

Cultural Events

Music, theater, dance, and art are popular throughout Iceland, even in the smallest communities. The country is home to a national theater company, the Icelandic Ballet Company,

As you might imagine, Icelanders enjoy many outdoor winter activities like skiing, sledding, and snowmobiling. During the country's brief summer, hiking, horseback riding, fishing, and hunting are also popular.

and the Iceland Symphony Orchestra. It is doubtful that any other city in the world can match Reykjavik in its per capita number of theaters, art galleries, musical performances, and other cultural activities. There are also many museums and festivals that preserve such traditional activities as woodcarving and weaving. While many Icelanders have achieved widespread recognition for their talents, none is better known than the pop singer Björk, who was born in Reykjavik and has gained international recognition.

Food and Dining

Iceland's Nobel Prize–winning author Halldor Laxness (in his *The Fish Can Sing*) described an early-twentieth-century banquet made up of "smoked lamb, pickled whale and sardines . . . steaming hot blood sausage . . . [and] singed sheep's heads." The country's diet, by some standards, is very bland and somewhat monotonous. Until recently, nearly everything eaten was produced locally; it was simply too expensive to import any but the most essential food-stuffs, such as sugar, coffee, and flour.

Fish is the mainstay of the Icelandic diet. Most people eat fish in some form at least once a day. It is eaten raw, pickled, smoked, or cooked in a variety of ways. Lamb and mutton are also popular meats. Boiled potatoes are served with most main meals, along with a boiled vegetable. Salads are rare, because most ingredients cannot be grown in Iceland. Dairy products are common; milk, ice cream, cheese, and yogurt are an important part of the diet. *Skyr* is a popular national dish similar to yogurt that is made from milk and eaten for breakfast, or as a dessert. Few spices, other than sugar and salt, are used in Icelandic cooking.

Traditional dining habits in Iceland are similar to those in the United States, with three meals a day the norm and dinner, which is usually served between 7:00 P.M. and 8:00 P.M., the largest meal. As also is true in the United States, as Icelandic families have become increasingly busy, the evening meal often is the only one at which all family members are together.

Icelanders are rightfully proud of their many accomplish-
ments, their heritage and traditions, and their high standard of
living. Although they are few in number and their homeland is
small, rugged, and located at the very edge of the inhabited
world, Icelanders have carved out a way of life that in many
respects is unsurpassed.

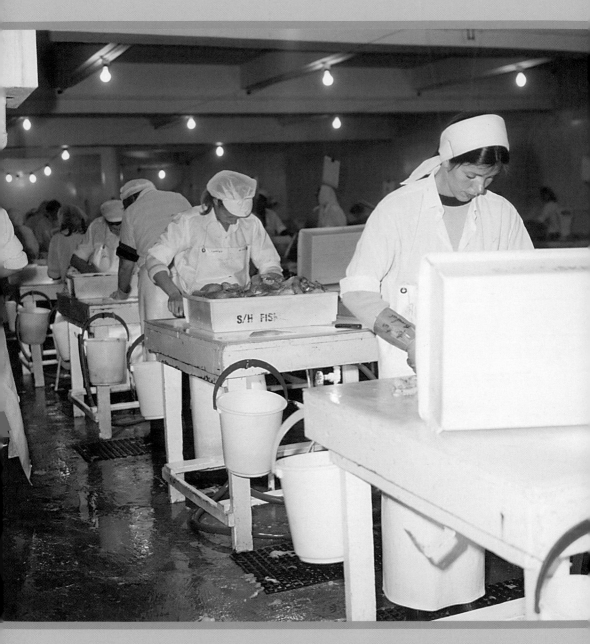

In the absence of most natural resources, Iceland depends heavily on fishing and fish processing, with more than 70 percent of the country's exports being marine products. Workers, like those shown here, have made Iceland a leader in these industries.

5

Economy
of Iceland

I celand's Scandinavian-type economy is basically capitalistic and similar to that of the United States and Canada. In addition, an extensive modern welfare system is in place. This covers the medical needs of the Icelandic people, with extensive medical, dental, and eye-care benefits. Free education (from preschool to the university level), guaranteed retirement pay, and high standards of living are also a part of this welfare system. Such cradle-to-grave public assistance does, however, come with a heavy price tag. Icelanders pay an income tax amounting to roughly half of their annual income, but at the same time illiteracy, poverty, prostitution, and violent crime are virtually unknown in modern Iceland.

On a per capita basis, Iceland is one of the wealthiest nations in the world. By nearly any measure, its people are very well-off. Joblessness is almost unknown, with more than 97.5 percent of the working-age population employed. This is due in part to the work ethic of the population and the progressive nature of the political system. Unlike the United States, there is a remarkably even distribution of income in Iceland. The Gross Domestic Product (GDP) purchasing power per capita was $28,710 (estimated) in the year 2000, and a typical family of four enjoys purchasing power of more than $100,000 (US). By comparison, the GDP purchasing power per capita for the United States in 1999 was $34,100. However, in the United States, incomes are less evenly distributed; some families are very poor while others are extremely wealthy.

FISHERIES

The country's ancestors were seafaring people and brought with them many ways of the sea, including fishing. Fishing and fish processing have been an important way of life throughout all of Iceland's history and continue to have an important position in the country's economy today. In the absence of other natural resources (except for abundant hydroelectric and geothermal power), Iceland's economy depends heavily on the fishing industry. Icelanders operate the fishing industry with a high degree of technology and skill, and are recognized worldwide as leaders in the industry. This industry, however, is very sensitive to declining fish stocks as well as to drops in world prices of fish.

Marine products make up more than 70 percent of the value of Iceland's exports. The rich marine life in Icelandic waters is the result of several conditions in the area's physical geography. One is the nature of the continental shelf, which is the generally flat, gently sloping surface of land beneath the sea which transitions from the coast to the deeper waters of the ocean. On this shallow continental shelf, the warm water of the Gulf Stream from the southwest meets the cold currents from the Arctic Ocean. These powerful oceanic currents, plus the relatively shallow water, create nutrients and temperatures that are ideal for marine life. Very few locations in the Northern Hemisphere have as favorable and rich fishing grounds.

This fisherman in Grindavik is unloading fresh cod from a fishing boat. In the past, dried fish was a mainstay of Iceland, but now most fish is processed and shipped all over the world.

About 12 percent of Iceland's work force is employed in the fishing industry. This includes not only the actual catching of the fish, but also processing the catch. To protect this industry, Iceland has imposed strict conservation measures, and fish catches are tightly controlled. Among the better known species of fish caught in Icelandic waters are cod, haddock, redfish, and herring.

Originally, fish were preserved by open-air drying. This was accomplished by erecting huge fish-drying racks constructed of vertical poles set in the ground, extending some 10 or more feet above the surface. These were then set in a gridlike fashion, much like the grid of a chessboard, about 15 feet apart. Horizontal poles were then attached near the tops of the vertical poles. The fish were split lengthwise, leaving the halves attached at the tail, and hung over the horizontal poles, much like hanging a towel over a clothesline. The horizontal poles were placed far enough above the land surface to prevent foxes and other creatures from reaching the fish. The fish would then be left on the racks to dehydrate for several months. Once they were dehydrated, the fish could be kept and stored for a long time, even in warmer climates. The consumer of dehydrated fish would reconstitute them by soaking them in water. The meat then could be cooked with vegetables.

Some dried fish is still produced in Iceland, but on a very limited basis. Once a common element of the cultural landscape, few fish-drying racks can be seen today. (Occasionally, a traveler may see a few fish hanging on a couple of poles.) Today, most of the fish are processed fresh and shipped to many parts of the world. Icelandic fish-processing plants have the most modern equipment, much of which is manufactured in Iceland. Most of the catch is filleted, packaged, and quick-frozen. Some fish is packed on ice and moved quickly, even by air, to markets in lands far from the seas of Iceland.

AGRICULTURE

Agriculture in Iceland has historically been very limited. Less than 1 percent of the land is arable (land that is fit for plowing or tilling) and used for the growing of crops. Perhaps no country in the world has proportionally less of its land suited for agriculture. Slightly less than one-fourth of the country is grass and meadowland suitable for grazing. The growing season— the period of time between killing frosts—is only three to four months. During this frost-free time, however, weather is generally cool and skies are often cloudy—neither condition ideal for raising crops. Most of the grazing land is used for growing grass for grazing and the cutting of hay.

Haying (making and putting up hay) is a very labor-intensive task in Iceland. Because of the humid climate and frequent precipitation, the hay must be turned several times to allow it to dry. It is then baled and wrapped completely in plastic to protect it from the weather. Much of the hay is used to feed sheep, dairy cattle, and horses during the long winter season. Some, however, is exported, primarily to Norway.

About 5 percent of Iceland's labor force is engaged in agriculture. In comparison, about 2.5 percent of the United States' labor force is in agriculture, fishing, and forestry. Thus, even though the total land area in Iceland used for agriculture is small, a larger proportion of the labor force is in agriculture than in many other countries. The farms are small and tend to be more labor-intensive than those in the United States, where large machines perform much of the work.

There are about 4,250 farms in Iceland, many of which have been in the same family for many generations. Even though they are small is size, the farms are usually located far apart.

Iceland is self-sufficient in the production of meat and dairy products. Sheep are the most important livestock and hay is the most important cultivated crop. The land is fertile enough to provide grass and other forage upon which farm livestock can graze. Other crops grown outdoors are potatoes, turnips, cabbage, and rhubarb, all on a very limited scale. In a few small valleys that are well protected from the weather elements, radishes, beets, and onions are also grown.

Because of the short growing season, the majority of Iceland's vegetables and some fruit are raised in commercial greenhouses. Tomatoes and cucumbers are the most common greenhouse vegetables. Geothermal water is tapped to heat the greenhouses and hydroelectric power provides the light. Most of these commercial greenhouses are located along the south coast in Hveragerdi, which means Garden of Hot Springs.

Some Icelanders have private thermally heated green-houses. In these, they raise vegetables, flowers, and other

Crowds flock to the annual sheep round-up in Skalholt, Iceland. This tradition dates to the Middle Ages. Wool and woolen products have provided Iceland with a much-sought-after export commodity. Icelandic sweaters, for instance, are world-famous for their distinctive designs and natural colors.

houseplants. Most of the island's people love flowers and this is one way they can have them year-round.

Sheep have been important to Iceland's economy since the days of the first settlement, and continue to be today. Because of the relatively cold climate, the sheep grow especially thick fleece, with longer outer hair covering much softer wool. The sheep, hence their wool, also come in many colors, including white, black, gray, brown, mixed, or patched. Because of these natural colors and the softness of the wool, Icelandic woolen goods are highly sought-after and quite expensive. Wool and woolen products have provided Iceland with a much-needed export commodity. Icelandic sweaters, with their wide variety of woven designs and natural colors, are world-famous.

Cattle are raised primarily as cows for milk. The major

Horses were originally brought to Iceland from Europe by the Vikings and Celts. The harsh Icelandic climate and selective breeding have caused them to evolve into smaller animals with heavier coats to guard against the cold. The horses shown here are direct descendants of those ridden by the Vikings centuries ago.

centers of milk production are located near the greatest con-centrations of people, since milk is a perishable commodity. One of these production centers is south of Reykjavik. Another is near the city of Akureyri on the northern part of the island. In addition to fluid milk, other dairy products are produced, including cheese, butter, *skyr*, cream, and ice cream.

Some pigs, chickens, ducks, turkeys, and pigeons also are raised on farms, but much of the grain fed to poultry must be imported. Because of the high cost associated with feed, poultry numbers are very limited.

Horses were brought to Iceland in the ninth and tenth centuries by the Vikings and Celts. These early horses were the ancestors of the present-day stock. Throughout the many centuries since the horse's first introduction, selective breeding and life in a harsh climate has resulted in a dramatic change in its make-up. Icelandic horses have evolved into a much smaller animal than their distant ancestors, with a much heavier coat. Its hair generally changes color in winter and becomes even more shaggy.

MANUFACTURING

Iceland's topography and climate have combined to make it one of Europe's richest nations in hydroelectric potential. The development of hydroelectric-generating stations providing cheap power has attracted foreign money and industry. Energy-intensive industries, such as aluminum smelting and ferrosilicon plants, have been attracted by this cheap power.

Bauxite, the ore that is ultimately turned into aluminum, is imported from Australia. This ore is processed in reduction plants, the largest located near Reykjavik. Even though the raw material must be imported, the country's cheap electrical energy makes it possible for Iceland to be a profitable producer of aluminum.

A ferrosilicon plant located on the west coast is owned jointly by the Icelandic government, Elkem A/S of Norway, and Sumitomo Corporation of Japan. This attests to the attraction that cheap power has for foreign investors. This plant also uses imported iron and silicon to produce the ferro-alloys used in the manufacture of steel.

Iceland has five medium-sized manufacturing enterprises whose plants produce fertilizer, cement, rock wool, algin products (for herbal health care), and salt. These plants make use of locally available raw materials and domestic sources of energy in their production processes. All require a high amount of heat and/or energy in their processing.

Seaweed is also a force in Iceland's economy; it is dried and used for fertilizing the soils on the farms. This requires a great amount of heat, but heat is cheap thanks to the geothermal resources of Iceland. Algin is produced from seaweed and used primarily as an herbal dietary supplement. Because the waters surrounding Iceland are virtually pollution free, this product is widely sought by health-conscious people around the world.

Salt is produced from brine by evaporating the water, leaving the salt residue. This requires an enormous amount of heat energy, which is cheaply and readily available in Iceland. The salt is used to preserve fish, remove ice from the highways, as a seasoning on food, and as an export commodity.

Cement, the bonding agent in concrete, is also produced in great quantities. Iceland is self-sufficient in this commodity, as it is in the manufacture of rock wool. Rock wool insulation is made by first heating basaltic rock to the melting point. The molten rock is then spun into long fibers, similar to our fiber-glass insulation, and used to insulate the buildings of Iceland.

Pumice is a very low density rock created by volcanic activity. A pumice rock will actually float on water because it is less dense than water. Iceland exports pumice primarily to the Scandinavian countries for the manufacture of aggregate blocks and chimneys. Pumice is also used in the blue-denim jeans industry to stone-wash jeans and other denim clothing to make them look old.

TOURISM

During the 1990s and early 2000s, the number of tourists visiting Iceland has increased dramatically. Iceland is only four to five hours by air from the eastern United States and even less from the European continent.

The chilliest thing about Iceland is its name. In January, the average temperature in Reykjavik, Iceland's capital, is higher that that in New York City. Almost everyone speaks

Iceland's raw and dramatic landscape is a sharp contrast to her modern cities. Each year, tourists from around the world visit the country to experience her geysers, hot springs, glaciers, and waterfalls, all of which are within driving distance of modern hotels.

English, and Icelanders are not really given to formalities. After all, a country that lists people by their first names in the telephone book cannot be overly formal and "stuffy"! In today's modern world, there are few opportunities to

Karl

Karl Bjarnason múrari Klettabg 34, 221 Hfj 555 2491, 865 6002
Karl K Bjarnason Vorsabæ 1, 110 Rey 567 2293, 852 5569
Karl Viðir Bjarnason Goðatúni 6a, 210 Gbæ ....⊠ 698 1843
Karl Þ Bjarnþórsson Einimel 19, 107 Rey 551 3613, 852 1209
Karl Björnsson húsasm Álfhólsvegi 66, 200 Kóp 554 0368
Karl Diðrik Björnsson Spóahöfða 26, 270 Mos 566 6973
Karl Blöndal blaðam Ásvallagötu 73, 101 Rey 552 4695
Karl Bóasson Suðurhvammi 18, 220 Hfj 565 3593, 892 5654
Karl Brandsson Öldutúni 16, 220 Hfj 555 4342
Karl Hermann Bridde bakarameistari
   Dverghömrum 36, 112 Rey 853 6595, 821 4777
KARL JÓHANN BRIDDE
   Víðinesi, 116 Rey **566 7890, 898 8207, 854 0128**
Karl Johan Brune rafeindav
   Snælandi 3, 108 Rey ....⊠ 553 1434, 899 7993
 - Netfang ....kbsh@mi.is
Karl Brynjólfsson sjóm Háabarði 10, 220 Hfj 565 1781
Karl Björgvin Brynjólfsson Giljaseli 4, 109 Rey 587 5858
Karl Gustav Carlsson Álftahólum 4, 111 Rey 891 6645
Karl Ómar Clausen Nesvegi 45, 107 Rey 551 1421
Karl Davíðsson Bakkasmára 20, 201 Kóp ....⊠ 554 4004

Because Icelanders are addressed by their first name, rather than their last, the Icelandic telephone directory may at first appear strange. Most Icelandic names are formed by adding "son" or "dottir" (daughter) to the first name of the person's father.

experience places that have remained little changed through the centuries and yet still be able to experience and enjoy a totally modern environment with all its amenities. This is possible in Iceland, however, where one can visit a world far removed from daily life, bond with nature, and feel a deep affinity with the past. At the same time, urban Iceland is modern in every respect.

Like most towns and cities in Iceland, the capital city, Reykjavik, is located near the coast. Many tourists are surprised to find the coastal city's setting lush, green, and nearly free of snow even during the winter months.

6

Visiting Iceland

Iceland has been discovered by visitors. The ease and relatively low cost of air travel, and the country's marvelous physical and cultural environments, have placed the island country on the map of tourist destinations. In this chapter, you will view Iceland through the eyes of a guest traveler.

GETTING THERE

Almost everyone who travels to Iceland will fly into Keflavik International Airport, which is located about 18 miles (30 kilometers) southwest of Reykjavik. This airport facility is actually a North Atlantic Treaty Organization (NATO) site maintained on Iceland. It also is home to Icelandair, the country's international airline.

Travelers to the country who expect to see only ice are in for a surprise. During a typical summer, more than 85 percent of the island is free of ice and snow. Most of the outer ring of Iceland, in fact, is lush green during summer months. Natural vegetation thrives because of the island's high amounts of rain and cool, but not frigidly cold, summer temperatures. A raincoat and a sweater, however, are essential items to pack for a visit to Iceland!

CURRENCY (MONEY)

The Icelandic monetary unit is the krona, made up of 100 aurar. The coins and notes in use are: 5, 10 and 50 aurar, and 1, 10, and 50 kronur coins. In late 2002, the conversion rate was approximately 88 Icelandic krona to 1 U.S. dollar. Credit cards are accepted by most major businesses in the larger communities.

LANGUAGE

While Icelanders speak a Scandinavian language called Icelandic, some knowledge of English is almost universal and most Icelanders also speak Danish, or some other Scandinavian language. French and German are also quite commonly spoken. Some of the older people do not converse in English as easily as the younger generation. Even in the small fishing villages far from Reykjavik, however, you will have very little difficulty communicating with the people.

REYKJAVIK

Nearly everyone traveling to Iceland will begin their visit in Reykjavik, the country's capital and largest city. Together with six surrounding municipalities, it forms what is commonly called the Greater Reykjavik Area. More than half of the country's population of 288,000 resides here. It is the home of the Althing—the Icelandic parliament—the Supreme Court, the National Theatre, the University of Iceland, the National Museum, and almost all major government agencies.

Reykjavik is the world's northernmost capital city. With only about 100,000 inhabitants (nearly 170,000 in the metro-politan area), it also ranks among the world's smallest capital cities. On the other hand, if you consider what Reykjavik has to offer in services, cultural life, and entertainment, it compares favorably with capital cities many times its size. Because of what Reykjavik has to offer, it has become known as "The Surprise City."

During the winter season, 25 to 30 concerts are given every month. Five to ten plays may be running simultaneously in theatres. The popular opera and the frequent art exhibitions add to the list of entertainment offerings. There are scores of restaurants to choose from that serve a variety of local, mainland European, and other international foods. Nightlife is very lively and numerous pubs, bars, coffee houses, discos, and ballrooms cater to different tastes and age groups.

GETTING AROUND

Organized tours of Iceland are available, but traveling by rental car is the best way to see the country. Driving your own vehicle gives you the freedom to travel places that organized tours do not visit. You also have the option of staying longer in an area if you choose. Car rental costs are high compared to those in the United States. Some savings can be had by renting a vehicle through a tour operator who offers a package that includes air travel, car rental, and even housing accommodations. Petrol (gasoline) is expensive, since it must all be imported. The 2002 price is over $1 per liter, or about $4.50 per gallon. For those planning to venture away from the capital, a four-wheel drive vehicle is essential. Icelanders drive on the right side of the road and with headlights on at all times. An excellent bus service links most communities, and larger towns and cities are reached by regularly scheduled commercial flights (Air Iceland and Icelandsflug) that are relatively inexpensive.

During the late spring, summer, and early autumn months, roads usually are clear (snow can fall during any month, however). The "Ring Road," Highway 1, was completed in 1974 and completely rings the island. Until 1974, it was not possible to

With large stretches unpaved, Iceland's Highway 1 may not seem like an engineering marvel, but it is. Construction of the road was completed in 1974 and required the building of many miles of bridges to span terrain flooded each year by glacial meltwater.

drive from the southwest portion of the island to the southeast portion except by taking the north loop. The reason no road ran east-west along the south edge of the island was the enormous amount of meltwater from the snowfields and glaciers that drains southward along the coastal plain. To construct a road here involved the building of tens of miles of bridges under which the meltwater could pass on its journey to the Atlantic. This was an enormous engineering feat and the construction costs were enormous. The majority of Highway 1 remains unpaved. It is more like a country gravel road on which one might travel in the United States. Erosion by rain and melting snow and ice has made this road surface very rough in places, and an occasional rock will protrude above the road bed. Rocks are constantly being exposed by erosion and frost action which pushes the stones toward the surface.

Following the 1996 earthquake within the Vatnajökull icecap in southeast Iceland, flights over the icecap discovered a subsidence bowl in the glacier surface at a location where a volcanic eruption had occurred in 1938. The size and depth of the subsidence bowl continued to increase. In addition, three more bowls formed, indicating intense melting at the base of the glacier. Searing hot lava was flowing upward under the ice causing the ice to melt and the glacier to subside. At the same time, the ice cover to the south started to rise. This indicated that meltwater from the eruption was flowing into the caldera depression and lifting the glacier. Huge quantities of meltwater continued to accumulate in the bowl-shaped caldera, causing the ice to rise even more.

The pressure of the meltwater eventually was sufficient to lift the glacier ice off the ground, causing the water to burst free in sudden torrential runoff. In the huge resulting flood, great volumes of water swept across the coastal plains, carrying with it 100 millions of tons of volcanic material and clay, and giant masses of ice weighing up to 1,000 tons. This sudden influx of water, ice, volcanic materials, and clay washed out many of the bridges on Highway 1. The highway remained closed for several months as the rebuilding of the bridges took place.

LODGING

Lodging is easily accessible in Iceland. Modern hotels provide comfortable accommodations in all of the larger communities. Winter rates are reasonable by U.S. standards; during the short summer tourist season, however, rates can be quite expensive. Information about facilities, rates, and availability is readily available on the Internet. As discussed earlier, many summer travelers to Iceland prefer to stay in schools.

DINING

The traveler to Iceland will find many restaurants, but he or she no doubt will be shocked at the cost of meals. Food prices are much higher than what we are used to in America, because most products must be imported. The typical hamburger, fries, and soda are available, as are more typical Icelandic foods like fish and lamb. Tipping is not expected in Iceland and, in fact, until several decades ago it was considered an insult to tip someone for services.

CRIME

Crime is not a large problem in Iceland (where could one hide?). It is common to see parents park their children in prams (strollers) on the street while they shop inside the store. This certainly would not be done in most large American cities. Homes and vehicles are often left unlocked. The lack of crime is just one of many reasons why Iceland ranks among the top few countries in the world in nearly all indices of human well-being.

ATTRACTIONS

Iceland has many interesting and often unique attractions. In chapter 2, mention was made of the country's many spectacular natural features. The island's rugged coasts, volcanoes, and glaciers are a "must" on the visitor's agenda. One will also find hot springs and hot tubs, the old fish-drying racks, Icelandic horses, and beautiful waterfalls.

One feature (or lack thereof) that surprises many visitors is that virtually all physical formations, even those that are potentially dangerous, are unfenced. There is an openness of these attractions that is foreign to Americans. You will not find protective fencing around the boiling hot springs, cascading waterfalls, steaming geysers, and other features. The people of Iceland are willing and able to take responsibility for their own actions. They do not need the protection of rails and fences to keep them away from potential dangers. Signs may be posted indicating the danger if you get too close, but no restraint is in place.

The Rettir

Iceland has more than half a million sheep—about two sheep for every person living on the island. The animals raised today are descendants of those brought to Iceland in open long-boats by Norsemen (Vikings) more than a thousand years ago.

During the summer season, the sheep graze on common lands. These common lands are natural pastures shared by groups of farmers; sheepherders are not needed. Every sheep has an ear tag, which identifies the farmer to whom it belongs. In the winter, the sheep are herded back to their respective farms, where they are fed hay and housed in barns.

Each fall, all the farmers who have sheep on this common grazing ground join together to gather in the sheep. The sheep are driven into an immense, wheellike stone sorting pen. This custom is referred to as the Rettir. The spokes of the wheel divide the pens into narrow, triangle-shaped areas. A large circular pen forms hub of the wheel.

This gathering of the sheep, or roundup, as we might call it, can take from one day to a full week. The time required depends on the distance that the sheep must be moved. Herding is done on horseback. Even though they are small, Icelandic horses are strong, and well-adapted to the rugged terrain and harsh climate. The common grazing land must be carefully scoured, because no sheep can survive the winter outside.

A lot of festivity accompanies the Rettir, which is an important social, as well as economic, event.

Travel and tourist information can be obtained from numerous Internet sources, either by topic, or by search under Website headings such as *Iceland travel information.*

As an independent republic, Iceland is less than 60 years old. But her history has shown her people to be intelligent, resilient, and independent. Despite the country's harsh climate and geographic isolation, her people maintain a thriving and enduring culture.

7

Iceland Looks Ahead

F or twelve centuries the people of Iceland have struggled against countless obstacles and won. There is ample reason to believe that they will continue to do so in the future. The country's natural resources are meager, yet on this small, remote, rugged island nation, Icelanders have developed one of the world's most enviable standards of living. Iceland is a peaceful nation. Its major battles have been against nature—the agents of fire, ice, and the sea—rather than other humans.

Forecasting the future of any country is, at best, an imprecise science. Geographers, however, do have a competitive edge in looking ahead. Their broad view of the world makes it possible to consider the importance of both physical and human elements of a place. These varied elements are analyzed in a number of ways. One view considers the many environmental interactions that give character to a place. In

Iceland, for example, geology, climate, and the sea have played a profound role in the development of a unique land and culture. Certainly, these elements will continue to be of great importance. Geographers also are keenly aware of the importance of space and time. In order to understand Iceland's past, present, and future, it is essential to consider the importance of its remote location. It also is essential to look to the country's past if one is to understand the present and draft a map to the future.

LIVING IN A HARSH LAND

Iceland is a harsh land. The history of its people is marked by their constant struggle against nature's elements. Nature's whims cannot be controlled. Humans can take steps to avoid or minimize the impact of natural hazards. As yet, however, we can not control earthquakes, volcanic eruptions, storms, or climatic changes. Of all the forecasts, perhaps the safest is to foresee a continuing fundamental relationship between Icelanders and their natural environment.

Earth Hazards

Aspects of environment, such as earthquakes and volcanoes, become hazards only in relation to human presence. Iceland's population is growing, settlement is expanding, and various types of development are occurring away from traditional population centers. These conditions suggest that conflicts between land and life will become increasingly frequent and severe. Earthquakes, volcanic eruptions, and periodic flooding caused by lava outbursts and melting glacial ice will continue to take their toll. No spot on the island is free from seismic (earthquake) activity, and most of Iceland is subject to the effects of volcanic eruptions.

Weather and Climate

Global warming could have a positive impact on Iceland's weather and climate. In late 2002, however, another—and much different—scenario was presented. Some scientists now believe that conditions in the North Atlantic Ocean are beginning to change. They fear that the North Atlantic Drift, the warm water extension of the Gulf Stream, may weaken or even disappear as a result of these changing conditions. Such changes, they caution, have occurred on a number of occasions, including during the historic period. And change can come very rapidly, in just a year or two. If this happened, eastern North America and Western Europe—and Iceland— could suddenly experience a 10°F (3°C) drop in temperature. Such a change would have a huge effect on Iceland, including a rapid expansion of area buried beneath glacial ice and permanent snowfields.

Glaciers

Glaciers remain somewhat of a mystery. Scientists are not sure, for example, whether they grow when conditions warm (contributing to more evaporation and precipitation), or cool! Even in the North Atlantic region, some glaciers are ablating (melting away) while others are growing (in Scandinavia, for example). It seems probable that whether Earth is warming, or the North Atlantic area is on the brink of rapid cooling, that Iceland's glaciers will experience some change in size and area covered.

Greater confidence can be expressed in terms of glacially caused flooding. Severe *jökulhlaups*, the flooding resulting from lava-caused glacial meltwater, will continue to pose a threat.

Vegetation

When the first European settlers arrived some 1,200 years ago, they described the island as being covered by dense forests. Because of extensive overcutting for lumber and fuel, nearly all the island's forests have been removed. Today, the government is supporting an ambitious program of reforestation. Also, as Iceland's population becomes increasingly urban, the importance of livestock grazing (particularly sheep) may decline. Sheep, in particular, tend to overgraze pastureland, which, in turn, can cause severe erosion.

The Sea

The warm waters of the north Atlantic Ocean are the source of Iceland's moisture and relatively mild climate. Should conditions change, as suggested in the discussion of "Weather and Climate" earlier, the impact on Iceland would be profound. In the past, most Icelanders have looked seaward for many of their needs. People came and went by sea. The sea provided their livelihood, as fishing dominated the nation's economy. Even ocean current–carried driftwood was gathered and used for fuel and building. Today, most people traveling between Iceland and a continental mainland do so by air. The country's economy also is changing. Nearly 75 percent of the labor force is engaged in manufacturing or providing services, and only 12 percent of the people rely on fishing and fish processing. In the future, Icelanders will be less dependent upon the sea for transportation or livelihood.

A STURDY PEOPLE LOOK AHEAD

Iceland's major strength, today and in the future, is its people. The population is healthy, well educated, socially integrated, and enjoys one of the world's highest standards of living. Few conflicts exist, whether within Iceland, or between the country and other lands. It is a peaceful country with little crime, little poverty, and little social diversity.

Geographers often speak of centrifugal versus centripetal forces—those conditions that can drive a society apart, or those that tend to draw it together. By nearly any measure, Iceland's population contributes to a centripetal force. The country's society is very cohesive and should remain so in the foreseeable future.

Population

Iceland's population of 286,000 is growing at a very slow and manageable 0.5 percent per year (versus the world average of 1.3 percent). Neither the current population, nor its rate of growth, poses a challenge to the country's area, economy, facilities, or services. In fact, Iceland appears to be one of the few countries on Earth that actually could benefit from population gain.

It is unlikely, however, that the island will experience any large or rapid gain in population. Most of Iceland's people are urban, educated, and affluent. And most women are in the work force. All four of these factors help contribute to a low birthrate and declining rate of natural population increase. It also is doubtful whether Iceland will gain many new immigrants. The island's natural environment and remote location work against attracting new settlers. So, too, do the high cost of living and very homogeneous population. Iceland's population should remain quite stable, experiencing slow growth that can easily be accommodated.

Government

Few countries in the world can match Iceland's political stability, a condition that almost certainly will continue. One question mark rising above the country is its possible future participation in the European Union (EU). For the time being, at least, Icelanders are happy to remain completely independent of this growing union of European countries.

Economy

Recent decades have seen a major shift in Iceland's economy. Traditionally, the people have turned to the land and sea for their resources and livelihood. Today, primary industrial activities such as farming, herding, mining, and fishing amount to but a small percentage of the national gross national

Iceland is very much part of the modern world. With an affluent and well-educated population, Iceland embraces new technologies and has made a smooth transition to an economy based more on services than manufacturing. Here, a young technician conducts DNA research at a biomedical firm.

product (GNP). Nearly all Icelanders—about two-thirds of the total work force—are engaged in service industries. A well-educated and hard-working population is Iceland's chief resource today. Certainly the importance of a variety of postindustrial service-based activities will increase. Iceland's economy appears to be on secure footing and should continue to diversify and grow in the foreseeable future. Short of some global cataclysm, only a devastating natural catastrophe could change this optimistic forecast.

LINKAGES

Even though Iceland is remote, it becomes increasingly less isolated. With jet aircraft, satellite and fiber optic communications, the Internet and e-mail, Iceland's location is no longer a major limiting factor to movement. People, materials, and information move to and from the island freely. Such linkages certainly will continue to improve in the future. This will encourage Iceland's population to be even move closely drawn into the global community.

LOOKING AHEAD

Geographer Erhardt Rostlund once said, "The present is the fruit of the past and contains the seeds of the future." Iceland's present has been fashioned by a sturdy people living in a harsh environment. Through their tireless work, determination in the face of adversity, and faith in themselves and their land, they have created a way of life that is first-rate by any world standard. By these efforts, Icelanders already have planted the seeds of their own future. And the results of their harvest almost certainly will be bountiful.

Facts at a Glance

Country name Conventional long form: Republic of Iceland

Location North Atlantic Ocean, west of Greenland and northeast of Great Britain and Ireland, roughly 64° to 66° North latitude and 14° to 24° West longitude. Geographically, statistically, and politically considered to be a part of Europe.

Area 39,769 square miles (103,000 square kilometers); slightly smaller than Kentucky and about the size of Virginia

Capital Reykjavik (population, 168,000)

Climate Maritime temperate; cool and moist, with conditions much warmer than would be expected for its location near the Arctic Circle; temperatures moderated by an arm of the Gulf Stream, the North Atlantic Drift

Land features Land is of volcanic origin; mainly rugged plateau surface with scattered low mountains; about 12% of the island covered by glacial ice and permanent snow, with the highest elevation being atop the glacier Vatnajokull (6,952 feet; 2,119 meters); rugged coast, with many fjords and bays

Natural resources Geothermal energy, hydroelectric energy, marine resources, spectacular scenery

Land use

No direct economic use	74%
Pasture	23%
Woodland	1%
Urban	<1%
Cropland	<1%

Natural hazards Earthquakes, volcanic eruptions, floods, blizzards

Nationality Icelander(s); adjective: Icelandic

Population 286,000 (2002 official); growing at an estimated .5% per year

Life expectancy at birth

Total population	80
Females	82
Males	78

Literacy Over 99% (the world's most literate country)

Ethnicity	Homogeneous mixture of Norse and Irish Celts
Language	Icelandic
Religion	Evangelical Lutheran (93%)
Independence	17 June 1944 (from Denmark)
Government	Constitutional republic
Chief of State	President
Subdivisions	23 *Syslur* (counties)
Currency	krona (in 2002, valued at approximately 88 krona to $1 US)

Labor force by occupation

Miscellaneous services	60%
Manufacturing	3%
Fishing & fish processing	12%
Construction	10%
Agriculture	5%

Industries	Fishing and fish processing, aluminum smelting, ferrosilicon production, geothermal and hydroelectric power, tourism
Gross domestic product	6.5 to 7.0 billion ($US)
Per capita GNP purchasing power parity	$28,710 (2001 est.)
Major exports	$2 billion: fish and fish products (70%), animal products, aluminum (European Union, 65%; U.S., 15%, Japan, 5%)
Major imports	$2.2 billion: machinery and equipment, petroleum products, foodstuffs, textiles (European Union, 56%, U.S., 11%, Norway, 10%)

Transportation

Highways	7,900 mi. (12,700 km); 2,030 mi. (3,270 km paved)
Railroads	None
Waterways	None
Airports	87 (12 with paved runways)

History at a Glance

20 million years Volcanic activity begins to create Iceland, a process that continues today.

c. 325 B.C. Greek explorer, Pytheas, reports venturing to a place named "Thule," which some believe to have been Iceland.

c. 700-800 A.D. Irish monks discover and settle in Iceland, a place known to Europeans as "Thule," a mysterious land at the northern edge of the known world.

c. 800 Norsemen discover Iceland.

874 Permanent settlement of Iceland begins by Scandinavian people from Norway, Sweden, and Denmark, and Celtic people from Ireland. First permanent settler, Norwegian Ingolfur Arnarson, builds his home in what is present-day Reykjavik.

874 Norse (Viking) sailors are able to make the difficult journey from Norway to Iceland in 7–8 days.

930 The "Althing," (Alping) Iceland's parliament, is established at Thingvellir. It marks the first time an entire country is ruled by a single national assembly and is believed to be the world's oldest governing parliament.

1000 Icelander Leif "Leif the Lucky" Eriksson discovers America and a names it "Vinland ." Law is passed by the Althing adopting Christianity as the official religion and requiring all Icelanders to accept the faith.

1117–1118 Icelandic laws are written.

1120–1300 Icelandic sagas, famous works of literature, are written.

1220–1262 Era of the Sturlings, named after a powerful Icelandic family; a period of turbulence.

1262 Weakened by internal conflict, Icelanders give up their independence to be ruled by the king of Norway (and later the king of Denmark). Foreign rule would continue until 1944.

1280 Iceland adopts new legal codes that remain in effect for centuries.

1380 Norway and Iceland become united with Denmark.

1300–1700 A time of great hardship. Disease, foreign exploitation, famine, taxes, and catastrophic volcanic eruptions devastate Iceland. Sharp decline in population to fewer than 40,000 people.

1530–1550	Protestant Reformation, Lutheran faith replaces Catholicism in Iceland. New Testament is translated into Icelandic in 1540.
1703	Iceland conducts national census of population, the first country to do so in the modern era.
1783–1784	Laki Volcano erupts in what proved to be Iceland's greatest natural disaster. Three-fourths of the island's livestock are killed and one-quarter of Iceland's people die of starvation.
1800	Danish king dissolves Althing and Icelanders begin to seek independence.
1843	Althing is reinstated as a consulting body, with Denmark retaining right to veto decisions.
1874	Iceland adopts own constitution and gains control of its own finances.
1904	Iceland is granted home rule, giving them their own government, but continuing to maintain strong ties to Denmark.
1911	University of Iceland is established.
1918	Denmark recognizes Iceland as an independent country, but the Danish king remains the Icelandic head of state.
1940	Denmark falls to Nazi German control and British troops occupy Iceland to protect the island from German invasion (in 1941, U. S. forces replaced British troops in defending Iceland).
1944	On June 17, Iceland declares itself a free and independent republic. Sveinn Bjornsson is elected president and a new constitution is adopted.
1945	Iceland's domestic airline makes first international flight.
1946	Iceland joins the United Nations.
1949	Iceland becomes a founding member of the North Atlantic Treaty Organization (NATO) with the understanding that it was not required to establish its own armed forces (in 1951, the United States assumed responsibility for Iceland's military defense).
1955	Iceland's Halldor Laxness receives Nobel Prize in literature.

1963   A four-year underwater volcanic eruption begins that creates a new island, named Surtsey, off the southwest coast near Heimaey Island in the Vestmannaeyjar (Westman Islands).

1973   Helgafell volcano erupts on the island of Heimaey. One-fourth of the island's houses are destroyed and many more are buried beneath tons of volcanic ash.

1974   Highway ("Ring Road") around the island is completed.

1975   Iceland claims exclusive fishing rights 200 miles from its shores. The United Kingdom starts "Cod War" in clashes between the British Royal Navy and the Icelandic Coast Guard.

1980   Vigdis Finnbogadottir becomes first woman in the world ever to be elected head of state in a democratic election (she was reelected in 1984, 1988, and 1992).

1985   Iceland declares itself a "nuclear-free zone."

1986   Reykjavik chosen as site of summit meeting between U. S. President Ronald Reagan and Soviet leader Mikhail Gorbachev.

1996   Devastating floods caused by volcanic eruption beneath the Vatnajokull (glacier) destroy highway and many bridges, plus homes and all else in its way, in southern Iceland.

Further Reading

Brigham Young University. *Republic of Iceland.* CultureGrams (annually updated), 1305 North Research Way, Bldg. K, Orem, Utah 84097-6200

Central Intelligence Agency. *CIA — The World Factbook, Iceland* (annually updated), *www.cia.gov/cia/publications/factbook/geos/ic.html*

Faces (People, Places, and Cultures). May 2000 issue of this Cobblestone Publishing Company magazine has 14 articles devoted to Iceland.

Hjalmarsson, Jon R. *History of Iceland: From the Settlement to the Present Day.* Reykjavik: Iceland Review, 1993.

Lacy, Terry G. *Ring of Seasons: Iceland — Its Culture and History.* Ann Arbor: University of Michigan Press, 1998.

Leiren, Terje I., and James Massengale (eds). *Faces: People, Places, and Cultures* (May 2000). Entire issue devoted to "Iceland," with 15 articles by numerous authors.

Lepthien, Emilie U. *Iceland.* Chicago: Children's Press, 1987.

Levathes, Louise E. "Iceland: Life Under the Glaciers," *National Geographic* 171:2 (February 1978), pp. 184–213.

Philpott, Don. *The Visitor's Guide to Iceland.* Ashbourne, England: Moorland Publishing Co. Ltd., current edition.

U. S. Department of State. *Background Note: Iceland* (annually updated), *http://www.state.gov/r/pa/ei/bgn/3396.htm*

Winter, Steve. "Iceland's Trial by Fire," *National Geographic* 191:5 (May 1997), pp. 58–71.

For further information on the country, contact the embassy of the Republic of Iceland, 1156 15th Street, NW, Suite 1200, Washington, DC 20005, or visit the Icelandic Foreign Service Website at *www.Iceland.org.*

Index

Index

Index

About the Author

ROGER K. SANDNESS is professor and head of the Department of Geography at South Dakota State University. He is in his fourth decade of college teaching and research. His main areas of interest are in physical geography, particularly landforms (geomorphology) and atmospheric science (meteorology). Roger has traveled extensively, including a month-long trip following Iceland's circle road route, to acquire a better understanding of the conditions of Earth's varied natural environments.

CHARLES F. "FRITZ" GRITZNER is Distinguished Professor of Geography at South Dakota State University. He is now in his fifth decade of college teaching and research. Much of his career work has focused on various aspects of cultural geography—how people live and what they do—and geographic education. Fritz has served as both president and executive director of the National Council for Geographic Education and has received the Council's highest award for his many contributions to geography education.